People are talking about...

"Short, insightful, often poignant, these prayers are truly 'off the cuff and from the heart.' John van Bemmel has tapped the everydayness of life and woven it into a pattern of words that bespeak the human condition of wonderment, search, and praise. A good take-with-you companion for all times and seasons. Recommended for all believing pilgrims."

Fr. William J. Bausch
Author, *A World of Stories for Preachers and Teachers*

"Van Bemmel's concrete and practical approach challenges us pray-ers to weave prayer more consistently and completely into the fabric of our lives. Prayer is living a relationship twenty-four hours a day, letting it express itself in the ache of loneliness as well as in the joy of dancing."

M. Basil Pennington, O.C.S.O.
St. Joseph's Abbey
Spencer, MA

"You *can* tell a book by its cover. At least this book. The words of the title say it well. What you see is what you get. All the prayers here are short and heartfelt... and are about everyday stuff. John van Bemmel doesn't just tell you about prayer, he prays—connecting with your emotions, everyday circumstances, needs for wonder and for worship... all 'good stuff.'"

Fr. Isaias "Ike" Powers, C.P.
Author of 14 books on gospel-oriented spirituality
including *Quiet Places With Jesus* and *Quiet Places With Mary*

"This book is a treasure that can usher you into greater intimacy with God. Drawing from the ordinary stuff of life, the author uses his own simple prayers to jump-start the prayer that already lives inside you waiting to be freed."

Macrina Wiederkehr, OSB
Author of *Gold in Your Memories*

"When a person goes deep into his or her innermost self, what is spoken touches everyone. This is what happens here. Every person who reads this book will be touched by something in it."

Rev. Gilbert Padilla
Author of *The Rain is Gone* and *Bits & Pieces*

"St. Paul says, 'Pray Always.' John van Bemmel shows how to do this in this collection. He proves that anything can be a springboard for prayer anytime: a news item, a feeling of depression, a stray thought, or a line of a Gershwin song. His words are spontaneous and simple. They are in line with St. Teresa of Avila's advice, 'Do not be bashful with so great a Lord.'"

Mary Kathleen Glavich, SND
Author of *Prayer-Moments for Every Day of the Year*

"Have you ever been in a stained glass studio? There's a lot of 'stuff' lying around: pieces of glass with various cuts, shapes, sizes, and colors. Amazingly, the artist will eventually fit these pieces together and produce a work of art. It's like that with this book. It offers a rich variety of prayer topics based on everyday life experiences, and YOU are to be the artist! YOU are to take this 'stuff' and turn it into prayer!"

William John Fitzgerald
Author of *A Contemporary Celtic Prayerbook*
and *Words of Comfort*

"When I first saw the title of Jack van Bemmel's book, *Prayers About Everyday Stuff*, I thought, 'Who needs another book of prayers?' But after reading only a few of the prayers, I was completely won over and found myself saying, 'I need a book of prayers—when the prayers are this good!' They are appealingly short, deceptively simple, and refreshingly straightforward. They remind us that any place is a good place to pray. I liked the tone of these prayers too. It's one I would call 'reverent familiarity.' This book is sure to lead many to pray more simply and honestly, 'off the cuff and from the heart.'"

Melannie Svoboda, SND
Author of *Everyday Epiphanies*
and *Rummaging for God*

Prayers about Everyday Stuff

off the Cuff and from the Heart

John van Bemmel

TWENTY-THIRD PUBLICATIONS

Mystic, CT 06355

Dedication

To Jamie, Laurie Beth, Kate, and Jennifer,
my son and daughters,
beautifully matured

Twenty-Third Publications
185 Willow Street
P.O. Box 180
Mystic, CT 06355
(860) 536-2611
(800) 321-0411

ISBN: 0-89622-968-8
Library of Congress Catalog Card Number: 98-61594
Printed in the U.S.A.

Contents

Introduction 1

teach me to pray 5
God of abundance 5
development 6
faith 6
listening to God 7
none to blame 8
Lent 8
human solidarity 9
healing ministry 10
God's presence 10
independence 11
adoration 12
Jesus of history 12
existence of God 13
death 14
why not? 14
God's will 15
consumerism 16
faith tradition 16
companionship 17
preaching the gospel 18
fidelity 18
love 19
parenting 20
Gandhi 20

the cosmic artist   21
respect for animals   22
the inescapable God   22
God's presence   23
resurrection   24
punishment   24
listening to God   25
church renewal   26
your precious word   26
silence   27
depression   28
God's revelation   28
grace   29
embracing adversity   30
human longing   30
doubts   31
the poor   32
conversion   32
wealth   33
prayer   34
Eucharist   34
God's presence   35
generosity   36
ingratitude   36
called by name   37
a tangible presence   38
compliments   38
war   39
near life's end   40
salvation   40
prodigal son   41
absence   42
inspiration   42

God's majesty 43
acquiring more 44
an authentic life 44
inertia 45
human family 46
perceptions of God 46
respect for creation 47
rights 48
incarnation 48
new life 49
relationships 50
soul mate 50
God's instrument 51
morality 52
forgiveness 52
God of paradox 53
the catalpa tree 54
have a good day 54
spirituality 55
seven times seven 56
rationalization 56
incarnate love 57
simple living 58
perfection 58
justice 59
you are near 60
food 60
confidence in God 61
Jesus 62
a delicate balance 62
mindfulness 63
providence 64
competition 64

invitation	65
sacramental reality	66
glorious beetles	66
discipleship	67
Christianity	68
priorities	68
church leadership	69
earth community	70
wisdom	70
multiplication	71
God's name	72
renewal	72
excuse me	73
abundant life	74
presence	74
God-talk	75
unity in faith	76
hills	76
thankfulness	77
honesty	78
witness	78
an observation	79
shrines	80
violence	80
gold and red leaves	81
worry	82
relaxation	82
suffering	83
a human life	84
obedience	84
love of neighbor	85
God's presence	86
living as art	86
sins of omission	87

Introduction

The fundamental purpose of prayer…is not to get something from God or to change God, but to change ourselves…the ultimate purpose of every kind of prayer is to give ourselves to God.
— Thomas Keating, O.S.C.O.

Many people value prayer in their busy lives and recognize its importance. As a rule and with a certain amount of ease they turn to God at the beginning and end of each day, often praying from a book of prayers, and at other times just letting their hearts speak. Occasionally circumstances prompt them to utter a spontaneous prayer, usually one of petition: at times of crisis and misfortune for themselves or others, when they are apprehensive or fearful, when they are grateful for blessings. Because they want to learn more about prayer and feel there is more to it than they have experienced, they are open to purchasing a book or pamphlet on prayer.

Prayers About Everyday Stuff is for people who already pray but may be somewhat dissatisfied with the way they pray or how often they pray. It is for people who want to expand the scope of their prayer and want to see more of a connection between daily life and their relationship with God.

A Way of Praying

This book of prayers has two realistic purposes. The first is to teach a process, or way, of praying, to facilitate prayer by opening up to pray-ers the rich world of subjects for their prayer, to point out that prayer can include more than asking God for "things" or thanking or praising God—however spiritually enriching that may be. The ambition of this book is to lead people who already pray to more frequent conversation with God about the stuff that really matters to them.

In addition to the ways mentioned above, pray-ers might consider these general occasions for prayer, that is, times when they might be moved to pray spontaneously:

- seeing anew or with a new slant something often seen before
- getting in touch with themselves in a new way
- being honest and forthright with themselves and with God
- frankly expressing to God their feelings and complaints, their joys and disappointments
- finding new meaning in an old saying or a familiar Scripture verse
- reflecting on an event in the news
- considering a recent experience or observation
- pausing on a spiritual truth that they see in a new light
- asking God questions about something that puzzles them
- following the promptings of the Holy Spirit.

The prayers in these pages are examples of prayer generated by such occasions. They include reflections, wonderings, observations, emotional stirrings, "insightings" that verbalize some of the many activities the human spirit is capable of. As such, they may occur at any time and place, and put pray-ers in not only daily but frequent contact with God. No subject, time, or place is off limits for prayer.

Praying like this may awaken in pray-ers a new and more profound sense of God's presence. If in their intimacy with God they share their thoughts and feelings with God on many subjects through the day, they will very likely become more conscious of God's abiding presence. Of course, there are appropriate times for more formal prayer, but praying in the way described here is for those other moments of the day, moments that are special and graced because they arise from the promptings of the Holy Spirit, as all genuine prayer does. Praying in this way may be described as "prayer off the cuff and from the heart."

The 125 prayers in this book are my own prayers over a period of time, the fruit of reflecting on a wide variety of daily experiences and expressing them to God, intimately, heart to heart. All pray-ers have generically similar experiences, even if they differ in details. Such experiences may, and should be, a significant basis of each one's prayer.

Prayer Starters

The second purpose of this book is to provide simple prayer starters. The pray-er may slowly read a prayer, reflect on it, and see if it resonates in any way in his or her soul. If it does, that person may make it his or her own to some extent and pray it, adapting it in any way to make it more appropriate. These prayers, which are on a multitude of subjects, may encourage pray-ers to try to pray in a similar way on their own when their feelings, disappointments, compassion, insights, joys, and the like move them to chat with God.

Throughout the book, there are lines to encourage pray-ers to add to the prayers, to write their own prayers on a stated topic or a similar one, or, where there is a felt need, to express agreement or disagreement with the printed prayer. The pray-er may also disregard the writing lines entirely and pray without them. If the content of any one prayer does inspire a person to pray—to praise God, question God, thank God, confess something, or complain to God—then the prayer has been eminently useful.

Of the two purposes described, the more important is the process embodied in all the prayers, not the content of any one prayer. In a word, each prayer individually may be used as a prayer prompter, a stimulus or take-off point for one's own prayer, and all the prayers taken together may be a guide to more frequent, more spontaneous, more honest, more varied prayer in God's presence.

Each prayer is addressed to God, although the word God is not used, but only implied by the word You (capital Y). Those who use this book, though, must feel free to address their prayers in any way they are comfortable with.

If prayer by its very nature makes us conscious of God's presence, then to pray often is to be often aware of the divine presence. Any event, any emotion may be an appropriate subject for prayer; nothing is entirely secular or outside the spiritual realm, and everything is a suitable subject for dialogue with God or for standing silently before God.

Those who pray regularly should be concerned not only with "my life of prayer," but with "my prayer of life." Such a grounding in everyday reality will lead to more abundant prayer.

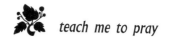 *teach me to pray*

"Teach us to pray,"
they implored Your son.
I too ask that You teach me to pray,
to be frequently in touch with You
and mindful of Your presence.
Books and counseling may guide me,
but above all I need Your Spirit
to draw me closer to You.
What can I do without You?

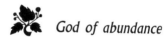 *God of abundance*

This morning of sleet and stiff winds,
several species of birds
that were numbered by the dozens
descended upon the backyard feeders.
I thank You for these
and praise You for their beauty
and wondrous variety.
They are an eloquent expression
of Your bounty.
You are, indeed, the God of abundance.

 *development*

Army ads invite us
to be all we can be,
and so do You.
When I meet You some day,
You won't want to know why I wasn't
Ignatius of Loyola or Mother Teresa,
but You will want to know why I wasn't
the person I could have been
by Your grace.

faith

As I journey along the road of faith,
You support me in many ways:
Your inspired word,
the witness of my ancestors,
the church and its celebrated sacraments,
the example of today's prophets.
But despite all this,
I am still a child
groping down the dark road of faith,
holding Your hand very tight.

 *listening to God*

Amid the clamor of daily life
on Main Street
I sometimes want to scream at You,
"Speak louder."

my prayer

_____

_____

_____

_____

_____

_____

_____

_____

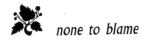 *none to blame*

If someone asked me to list
all my complaints against You,
I honestly wouldn't know where to begin,
not that I have too many complaints,
but that I have none—really!
I can't blame You for my circumstances,
my failure, sorrows, and losses,
nor even for this imperfect world
and its disasters.

 Lent

I pray this Lent
that You will give me the courage
to do what I should to serve You better
in my brothers and sisters.
But first grace me with the honesty
to see myself for what I am,
not with the mask I wear for others to see.
Let that be the starting point—
the real me that You see—
of my conversion.

 *human solidarity*

As I sit in soulful silence
in an empty church,
I feel the comforting presence
of countless brothers and sisters
You have given me.

my prayer

 *healing ministry*

As I walk the corridors of the cancer center,
I see Jesus still working among us.
Through technicians, doctors, and nurses
he carries on his ministry,
healing every kind of sickness.
Thank You for his ongoing presence.
Help me to value the sacred work
these people do.
Inspire me to be a healer
when someone in Your family
is in need of healing,
emotional or physical,
and transformation.

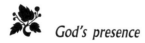 *God's presence*

As I lie awake in the early morning hours,
listening to the endless ticking
of the tall-case clock,
I know You are with me.
That is how You are,
and it comforts me.

 *independence*

My granddaughter is beginning to show signs
of a healthy independence
of her parents.
Sometimes I think that is how
You want me to be,
to mature in Your sight.

my prayer

_____

_____

_____

_____

_____

_____

_____

 *adoration*

How odd that the word once used
only for You
should now be the pop term
we reserve for fashions,
handsome actors, and kittens.
It is never used for You any more;
we seem to be embarrassed to utter the word
in Your regard.
But I will dare to use it
with its exclusive meaning:
I adore You.

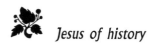 *Jesus of history*

When I observe how splintered
Your son's church has become,
how suspicious and untrusting its members,
how incompatible
the Christ each splinter professes,
I feel more driven to seek
the Jesus who walked Palestine's roads
and urged us to be one in love.

 *existence of God*

A theologian used to say,
"What matters is not whether God exists"—
that's an abstract God—
"but whether God is with us."
That's the most meaningful question
we can ask,
the only one that matters.

my prayer

_____

_____

_____

_____

_____

_____

_____

_____

death

You know all my thoughts and wonderings,
even those that are "undoctrinal."
Here's one of them:
Is death
only the sting of wrenching separation
from loved ones,
or will I also find myself enfolded in the love
of Your warm embrace?

 *why not?*

You must be used to us
shaking our fists at You,
screaming, "Why me?"
"Why now?"
"Why here?"
but do we ever think,
"Why not?"

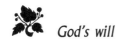 *God's will*

"Your will be done...."
In theory, I really have little problem
in wanting to follow Your will.
The problem,
in this very gray world,
is in recognizing it.
Grant me keen discernment
and a courageous heart to do Your will.

my prayer

_____

_____

_____

_____

_____

_____

_____

_____

 *consumerism*

Pop culture and Madison Avenue
are trying their mightiest
to supplant Your way with theirs,
to eradicate gospel values for their own,
and to convince me
that consumerism,
which would eventually consume me,
is the only way to lasting satisfaction.

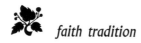 *faith tradition*

During the entrance procession
of a eucharistic celebration,
Your grace touched me, almost tangibly:
I saw myself as
part of a long faith tradition,
grateful to be a link in the long chain
of those who serve You
in this family of faith;
indebted to those
who brought me Your love and Your church.

 *companionship*

"With rue my heart is laden
for golden friends I had…."
I thank You for enriching my life
with worthy, faithful friends.
My advancing years make it clear, though,
that I am going to face increasing loneliness.
Be my lifelong companion.

my prayer

preaching the gospel

The legend is that Francis said
we are to preach the gospel every day—
even if we have to use words.
Only You and he would know if he said that,
but he couldn't have been the first.
The message is too crucial to the gospel
to have gone unsaid for a thousand years:
The first and most effective way
I preach Jesus
is by the way I live each day.

fidelity

"This above all: to thine own self be true…"
Grant that I may also be true
to my nature,
to my environment,
to all others,
and to You, as You ever are to me.

love

Do I,
like the rich young man,
pride myself on observing the law,
or do I strive to embrace
Your self-forgetting law of love?

my prayer

_____

_____

_____

_____

_____

_____

_____

_____

parenting

I hear parents protest about how difficult
it is to bring up children today.
It does seem more difficult
than when I was actively parenting.
I pray that You support these parents.
By Your grace, may they inspire their children,
as they mature,
to move with the culture around them—
up to a point—
but in the end, to work to change
the culture around them.

Gandhi

I thank You for Your prophet
who taught us respect for nature
and love for all humanity,
who showed us the nonviolent way
to resolve our deepest differences.
Thank You for Mohandas Gandhi,
the great-souled one.

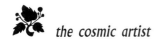 *the cosmic artist*

If the poet Millay revels,

"O world, I cannot hold thee close enough,"

does she see in it

the reflection of Your beauty,

the revelation of Your presence,

your very Self?

You, the cosmic artist,

have poured Yourself into Your work.

my prayer

_____

_____

_____

_____

_____

_____

_____

_____

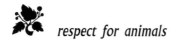 *respect for animals*

Your animals!
Is this what You intended?
Somehow we think You created them
solely for our amusement
(not for theirs, surely):
rodeos, bullfights, races, fashion,
circuses, hunting for sport.
In Your creation we may be superior
in some respects,
but not so that we may use them
any way that pleases us.

 the inescapable God

You are the inescapable God.
"You have searched me and known me...
and are acquainted with all my ways....
You hem me in, behind and before."
Some may shake a fist at You
and protest that this is
the worst news possible,
but this is the ultimate good news—isn't it?

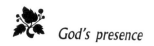 *God's presence*

I stretch out my arm into infinity
to touch You,
but then I feel Your abiding presence
right next to me.

my prayer

_____

_____

_____

_____

_____

_____

_____

_____

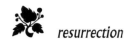

resurrection

I rejoice to think of Your plans for me, for us.
Will you really raise me up on eagle's wings
and bring me to Yourself?
Until then, by your grace,
let me
live to be worthy
of this final union with You
and with all who have loved You.

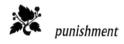

punishment

I have heard people declare
that the horrible death from AIDS
is punishment for the "obvious" sin.
How grotesque for anyone to think that of You!
They and I have very different images of You.
How can anyone even suspect that any evil
is Your punishment for a particular sin?
We know for certain that You are love;
how or when or if you punish us in this life
is up to You, only for you to know.

 *listening to God*

You are never at a loss for words;
You speak to me in what You have created,
through Your holy book,
through Your prophets and other people,
and in the signs of the times.
Trouble is, I'm not always listening.

my prayer

_____

_____

_____

_____

_____

_____

_____

_____

church renewal

It's so disheartening to read about
the decrees and directives from Rome.
They seem to have lost a true pastoral sense,
the compassion and understanding
we expect from those who
minister in Jesus' name.
Not to lose hope, though.
Renew in all of us the spirit of the gospel
and grant us fresh insight
for Your kingdom's sake.

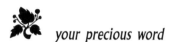

your precious word

At Mass I was deeply struck
by something that I had seen
countless times before:
the entrance procession with
the lector processing to the sanctuary,
solemnly holding the lectionary on high,
Your word to feed us through life.
Let me grasp more of your precious word
in a fresh way.

 *silence*

At this early morning hour
my mind and heart are drawn to You,
not to say anything, really,
but just to sit here
and humbly soak up Your serene presence.
Who needs anything more?

my prayer

_____

_____

_____

_____

_____

_____

_____

_____

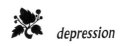 *depression*

Some days, like today,
even when the weather is beautiful
and no particular problem haunts me,
I feel a dark cloud over me;
it's hard to smile
and there's little relish for life.
I'm just going through the motions.
And worse, I ask myself,
where are You?
If only Your presence were consolation
when nothing else is.

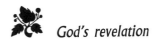 *God's revelation*

When I reflect on the first nanoseconds
of the Big Bang,
I wonder,
isn't that the first page
of the story of Your self-revelation?

grace

I know from my own experience
and Your holy Scripture
that grace abounds.
What I do not seem to appreciate
and praise You for
is that You are free to channel Your grace
in strange, surprising ways.
Who am I to restrict
the time, place, and medium
You use to touch my mind and heart,
or anyone else's?

my prayer

 *embracing adversity*

"Cancer is a word, not a sentence,"
the hospital sign said
with clever encouragement.
Instill in her, I pray,
true patience and steeled determination,
saving good humor and unshakable hope.
Heal her and grant cleansing remission.
She has, for her family—
and who knows who else?—
been a model for embracing adversity.
I thank You for her,
and for her costly example
of grace under fire.

 *human longing*

Are our human sexual longings
somehow a shadow manifestation
of our restless hearts
longing for You?

 *doubts*

When doubts about You and Your ways
suffocate me,
I take comfort in thinking
that at least
You are on my mind.

my prayer

_____

_____

_____

_____

_____

_____

_____

 *the poor*

"Glory to God in the lowest,"
as your servant Chesterton prayed.
I pray that I may see You
among the poor,
among the defenseless and despised,
among those who thirst
that justice may be done on their behalf.
May they always give You glory.
Let me be, like Jesus,
a friend of the poor—in deed.

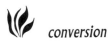 *conversion*

Have You not provided for everyone
a moment of grace,
a pivotal experience of conversion
a unique exodus event in life,
when You offer to lead them
from bondage—
attachment—
to full liberty as children of God?

wealth

Here's the question I'm afraid to ask;
I don't want to hear the answer.
How much wealth is enough for me?
Or worse, is there ever enough?
Enlighten me to see all this
through Your eyes,
to see where real wealth lies.
Can I live by the Middle East proverb,
"Enough is a feast"?

my prayer

_____

_____

_____

_____

_____

_____

_____

_____

prayer

Your holy word tells us
to ask for what we need,
but has asking for things
become the only element—
the heart—
of my prayer?

 *Eucharist*

"Do this in memory of me."
After I leave a eucharistic celebration,
what can I do
in memory of Your son
so that I can bring the Eucharist
to my daily life
and my daily life to the Eucharist?
Transform me so that everything I do
may be my response to Jesus' command.

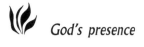 *God's presence*

You stand apart
in ineffable and awesome holiness,
but You allow me
to call You by Your name:
the One Who Is Always Present.

my prayer

_____

_____

_____

_____

_____

_____

_____

_____

 *generosity*

Like Your spirit hovering above the waters
when You created the world,
Your spirit was recently seen
again at work over raging waters,
as neighbors labored night and day
to help their flooded neighbors.
Thank You for creating generous, giving hearts.

 *ingratitude*

Like my four-year-old grandson
who, wide-eyed,
holds his ears when he is embarrassed,
I can picture myself standing like that
before You,
forgiven by Your grace,
but embarrassed at the sheer ingratitude
of my behavior.

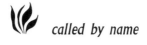 *called by name*

You,
the incomprehensible one,
the divine enigma,
the totally other,
absolute reality,
You call me by name.
I stand before You,
astonished and abashed.

my prayer

_____

_____

_____

_____

_____

_____

_____

a tangible presence

When a friend or stranger
feeds me,
visits me,
consoles me,
heals me,
or forgives me,
Your caring presence
becomes authentic and tangible.

compliments

I discovered something today,
something I should have detected long ago.
It's a blessing I thank You for.
How easy it is to compliment people;
how much it means to them.
I told a man painting a lamppost
that he was doing a good job (he was);
I mentioned to an employee at the market
that she did a great job
packing groceries (she did).
They lit up.
Open my eyes to the good around me.

war

What must You make out of
this great irony of the ages,
that those who believe in You
and in the Prince of Peace
have waged wars of conquest and oppression
against one another
in Your name?

my prayer

_____

_____

_____

_____

_____

_____

_____

_____

_____

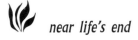 *near life's end*

As the candle of my life
is beginning to burn low,
I think more frequently of You
and meeting You.
At the same time,
while I am not fond of the thought of dying,
I don't fear it either.
Help me to embrace it
when it comes.

 *salvation*

Hearing this Gershwin song
makes me think of You.
What a blessing it is to have
"someone to watch over me."
Not that You will keep me
from all physical danger while I live,
but that You will help me to avoid moral evil
and above all, the ultimate evil:
being forever separated from Your love.

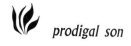 *prodigal son*

There's a phrase in Jesus' story
of the prodigal son
that stands out in my heart,
one that says more to me
about You
than whole chapters of Scripture:
"…while he was yet a far way off."

my prayer

_____

_____

_____

_____

_____

_____

_____

_____

 *absence*

Deep depression must be
when I feel the heavy absence
of incarnate love,
when I feel Your absence.
Is this my "dark night of the soul"?

 *inspiration*

You inspired the writers of the Bible,
revealing Yourself,
guiding us to truth,
sketching out for us
how we are to live.
It is hard to believe
that You did not, in some way,
inspire the sacred books
of other faiths as well.

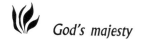 *God's majesty*

When I read that the stars
of Your expanding universe
are more numerous than all the grains of sand
on this planet's beaches,
I am swallowed up in awe
of Your creative, majestic presence.

my prayer

_____

_____

_____

_____

_____

_____

_____

_____

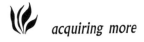

acquiring more

Will I ever reach a point
where the sole motive
for my desire to acquire
more of this world's goods
is so I can better do Your work?
My past experience tells me that I won't,
but that is selling you short,
isn't it?

an authentic life

"Get a life," I hear people saying,
often with ridicule and superiority,
as if putting the engine of ambition
into high gear
or buying chic items
will enrich life
automatically and immeasurably.
Never let me forget what life really is
in Your sight,
and how I should live it
in Your company.

inertia

When I consider the heroism
of this world's prophets
in championing the poor
and protesting injustice,
I'm ashamed to ask myself
why I remain a potted plant
on the stage of social activism.

my prayer

human family

If family is so important to us
and feeds our emotional needs,
should I not include in my love and concern
all the human family,
all who come from Your hand,
as my sisters and brothers?

perceptions of God

My diverse experiences in life—
my reflection and prayer and study,
Your Spirit's work in my heart—
all these lead me to think it's true,
that each person has a different image of You,
worships a different god.
You are one person's god—
this person's.
And at the same time,
I stand in solidarity with all
who worship You.

respect for creation

I rejoice that I am part of nature
and do not stand apart from it.
I am honored to be related
to all that You have created.
You have created us to co-exist
for our mutual benefit.
Let my respect for nature
be my thanks to You.

my prayer

_____

_____

_____

_____

_____

_____

_____

_____

rights

In a society caught up
with "my rights,"
I smile to think that there is nothing
in my relationship with You
that I can claim as my right,
not Your creating me and calling me by name,
not Your holding me in existence,
not Your loving presence or boundless mercy.
Nothing.
All this, like You Yourself, is gift.

incarnation

Jesus was a storyteller
and his life was a story.
I can measure the story of my life
against his.
Whoever sees Jesus sees You.
But what if there were no Jesus?
How would I know You then?
You wouldn't have a story I could understand.
Thank You for the supreme gift of Jesus.

 *new life*

My daughter invited me
to be at the birth
of the child she is carrying.
Thank You for this exquisite opportunity
to witness Your life and love
passed on to another child of Yours.
To me,
it is a harbinger of resurrection.

my prayer

_____

_____

_____

_____

_____

_____

_____

_____

 *relationships*

Once you have created me
in Your image and likeness,
it is part of my very fiber
to be in a relationship with You,
the Holy Trinity
and parent of us all,
and with people everywhere.

 *soul mate*

I awake each day to discover anew,
beside me,
Your wonderful gift to me.
She is my intimate companion through life,
the half of my soul.
We are "so both and oneful."
What does such a relationship
teach me about You
and the love You bear us all?

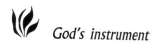 *God's instrument*

"Make me an instrument of Your peace…"
of Your compassion,
of Your tolerance,
of Your forgiveness,
of Your mercy,
of Your love.
Together, we can make Your reign
more tangible.

my prayer

_____

_____

_____

_____

_____

_____

_____

_____

 *morality*

Each day,
in large and small matters,
I make decisions
between doing what is moral
and what is not,
striving to please You.
Bless me with increased sensitivity
to Your call
so that I may also strive
to choose the better over the good.

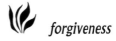 *forgiveness*

When the Christmas choir sang,
"The grace of God has appeared,"
I thought of Your Spirit
at work in my heart,
calling me, Your prodigal son,
back to Your forgiving arms.
By Your grace,
let me not stray from You
ever again.

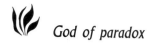

God of paradox

You are a god of paradoxes:
eternal and with me in time,
distant and immanent,
fiercely righteous and ever forgiving.

my prayer

_____

_____

_____

_____

_____

_____

_____

_____

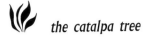

the catalpa tree

If the catalpa tree is Your creation
and the manifestation of Your bounty
and Your presence,
why would I not want to hug it
and think of it,
as Francis might have,
as Brother Tree?

have a good day

Many people tell me to have a good day.
I wonder what they mean by it,
if they mean anything at all.
The question is,
what do I think a good day is?
At each day's end,
You are the yardstick to judge
if the day has been good or not.
The love I have shown
and the good I have done—
there's where the true answer lies.

 *spirituality*

I know spirituality is important,
but the word is vague and mystifying,
something reserved for "holy people"—
except when I think of it
as my concrete, day-to-day
relationship with You.

my prayer

_____

_____

_____

_____

_____

_____

_____

_____

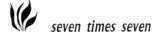 *seven times seven*

You make my scarlet sins
as white as snow;
You forgive me seven times seven.
You are great indeed!
Grace me with a penitential heart.

 *rationalization*

When disaster strikes someone,
why are people prone to assign
the cause to You,
as so much deserved punishment
for a particular sin?
We can never know
what is punishment from Your hand.
That is Your business, not ours.

 *incarnate love*

I thank You for all the world's people,
because without them,
how would I show my love for You
in a concrete way,
and how would You show Your love for me?
You and I love each other
through others.

my prayer

_____

_____

_____

_____

_____

_____

_____

_____

simple living

The great error of our culture
is that we think we can satisfy
our deepest yearnings
with unrestrained consumerism.
I will discover myself and You
when I live more simply
and liberate myself from this luggage
that distracts me and weighs me down.

perfection

How many people have been discouraged
by that gospel exhortation
to be "perfect," as You are?
A cold, misleading translation
has saddled us with false expectations.
Aren't we, rather,
called to the fullness of life,
called to be entirely devoted to You?

justice

To listen to some people
talk about everyday life and Your holy book,
You would think the Bible abounded
with ordinances about sex,
with hardly a word about justice.
Just the opposite.

my prayer

_____

_____

_____

_____

_____

_____

_____

_____

_____

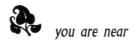

you are near

Some days, in a moment
of heightened awareness of Your nearness,
my heart sings at the thought of You;
other days, if I think of You at all,
it is in passing
and with little personal concern.
Either way, you are still with me.

food

How common and fitting
to thank You at meals for the food we eat.
But thanks as well for the many
who labor to bring the food to us:
the baker and butcher,
the crop picker, farmer, and trucker,
the processor and shopkeeper.
Bless their work and be mindful
of those who are underpaid
and mistreated in their work.

 *confidence in God*

Whatever "resurrection of the body"
may mean,
I know that nothing undesired
will befall me
when at last You call me to Yourself.

my prayer

_____

_____

_____

_____

_____

_____

_____

_____

Jesus

You know what I admire about Jesus?
He recognized authority
but stood up to it courageously
when he thought it unjust.
He was single-minded
and committed to his priorities.
He befriended the poor and defended them,
even when it cost him.
With him,
what you saw was what you got.
Just thought I'd mention it.

 a delicate balance

One immense task I have
along the unending road toward maturity
is to balance
Your invitation to trust You
and be a person of faith,
with the use of the intellect You gave me.

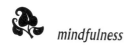 *mindfulness*

The soul of my prayer
is to stand before You,
silent and confident,
mindful of Your enveloping presence.

my prayer

_____

_____

_____

_____

_____

_____

_____

_____

_____

 *providence*

Listening to the thin voices
of the grade school choir,
I think how different
the life story of each child will be,
and of the various ways
You will be present in the world
through them,
their many gifts used in Your service,
until you bring them back to Yourself.

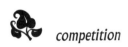 *competition*

I live in a culture
that is obsessed with competition.
Almost nothing is done without it.
Why must we educate
by pitting one child against another?
Can we not sport
by seeing what we can accomplish together?
Is having "winners" and "losers"
part of Your scheme of things?

 *invitation*

What an utterly remarkable enterprise
I am involved in:
called into a relationship
of friendship with You,
invited to share in Your life forever—
all given to me gratis.

my prayer

_____

_____

_____

_____

_____

_____

_____

_____

sacramental reality

What a narrow understanding of sacrament
I was raised on,
right into adulthood.
But education is ongoing,
and I see now the richness of this notion:
that all of reality is sacramental,
the bearer of Your presence,
the instrument of Your saving activity.

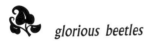
glorious beetles

Humans created in Your image
give You glory,
as St. Irenaeus told us long ago.
But among all Your creatures,
I like to think of beetles (of all things)
giving You glory.
Because of their improbable numbers,
diversity, and capabilities,
not to mention their necessity for this planet,
they glorify You
and in their own way chant Your praises.

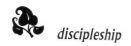 *discipleship*

To be honest with You,
I shudder to think what it would really mean
were I to serve You
and my brothers and sisters
the way Jesus challenges me to.
Have I chosen, instead,
to follow the way
of a convenient, accommodated Christianity?

my prayer

_____

_____

_____

_____

_____

_____

_____

 *Christianity*

I wonder how many Christians
really take their religious faith
at face value,
ready to embrace the sacrifices
it may require,
and follow the exacting example of Jesus,
living each day for others,
and not compromising to society's values.

priorities

How revealing, I thought;
someone recently called shopping malls
the cathedrals of our time.
They are monuments to our boundless desire
for more than we need for wholesome living.
Instill in me the desire to live more simply
so that others may simply live.
By Your grace,
let me learn the difference
between "want" and "need,"
and rearrange my priorities.

 *church leadership*

Lately I am deeply disappointed
in church leadership,
especially at the Vatican level.
How hard it is to recognize
in their words and deeds
the ministry of Jesus;
how hard at times to reconcile
their leadership
with Your call to a ministry of service.

my prayer

_____

_____

_____

_____

_____

_____

_____

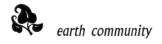

earth community

How good it is to recognize my place
among my sisters and brothers,
people the world over,
whether believers or not.
But, thanks to Your mind-opening grace,
I've come to see that I am related
to all this planet's creatures.
I am one of them,
one with them,
part of the "nature" You created.

wisdom

Teach me true wisdom,
I pray You,
the wisdom that comes
from my daily experiences.
Help me to be alert to each day's events,
my thoughts and deeds and feelings,
so that I may see beyond the surface
and learn from them
the deeper meaning of life
and grow more familiar with Your ways.

 *multiplication*

You must have loved the poor,
a wag once observed,
because You made so many of them.
I am saddened to inform You
that their number is growing
by leaps and bounds
every year.

my prayer

_____

_____

_____

_____

_____

_____

_____

_____

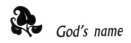 *God's name*

To the philosophers,
You are the faceless god
who is all-this and all-that,
but as the god who has revealed Self,
You are the indescribable one
whose name is With-You.

 *renewal*

Folding laundry and washing the car,
repainting the hall and sweeping the walk,
recovery from illness and depression—
all instances of renewal, of starting over,
every day, in all areas of my life.
Let these be my daily reminders
to turn to You often
in repentance,
with the firm hope of rebirth
in Your good favor.
Be the spark of our rekindled relationship.

 *excuse me*

At my baptism
You anointed me Your prophet,
as You did Jesus at his baptism.
But from what I know about prophets,
Jesus included—
the threats and derision they are subject to—
I ask You to hold this coward
excused.

my prayer

abundant life

This paltry pond teems with life:
bass, peep frogs, and black snakes,
water skimmers and dragonflies;
nearby in the trees many species of birds;
white tail deer that come for water,
as do the wild turkeys;
herons and mallards that visit occasionally—
all of them my fellow creatures.
And what would a microscope show me?
In this small corner of creation
You are present,
sustaining abundant life.
Thank You.

presence

As unexpectedly as a sparrow
that settles at my feet,
tilts it head and looks at me
as I sit quietly on a terrace,
so does the thought of Your loving presence
settle on my soul.

 *God–talk*

You have to be amused
at the dispute going on
about the language we are to use
when we speak and write about You.
Do we use "he" and "him"?
"She," "her"?
Call You "mother-father"
or "parent"?
or "Godself"?

my prayer

_____

_____

_____

_____

_____

_____

_____

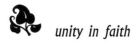 *unity in faith*

It is so distressful
to see the disagreements,
the bitter disputes and want of charity,
the mistrust and name-calling,
the rigidity and condemnations
among some of those who believe in You,
in Your son, and in his church.
I pray that we may all appreciate
not so much our differences,
but the riches we share
in our common faith.

 hills

On the summit on a warm spring day,
I gaze over the expanse of hills,
running green to gray to purple
as they stretch to the horizon,
and I want to ask You, the creator,
"What must You be like?"

 *thankfulness*

The cloudless sky and soothing breeze,
the vast expanse of white-capped ocean,
the strident gulls and teeming tidal pools,
the surf crashing against the rock-lined shore—
I thank You for these.
They take my breath away.
Breathe ever deeper gratitude
into my thankless heart.

my prayer

_____

_____

_____

_____

_____

_____

_____

_____

_____

 *honesty*

Having heard my son
caution his child about lying,
I rush to pray for rigorous honesty.
By Your grace,
I want to avoid the deceit
that may be
the most unhealthy and harmful of all:
the lie I may tell
about myself,
to myself.

 witness

Here's a blunt and demanding question
that Jesus' testimony in John—
"Whoever sees me
sees the one who sent me"—
brings to mind.
Over a period of time,
would people be able to tell
from the way I live
that You have sent me
to do Your work?

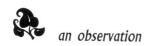 *an observation*

It takes an "outsider" to see
to what we have grown blind.
Your good servant Mohandas Gandhi's comment
should make us very sad, even ashamed,
to think how poorly we have followed
Your son's charter:
"Much of what passes today as Christianity
is a negation of the Sermon on the Mount."

my prayer

 *shrines*

Do I have any shrines in my life?
Not out-and-out religious shrines,
such as at Lourdes
or the candlelit shrines in some homes,
but the personal places or things
that enrich me spiritually,
fill me with reverence,
hold an enchantment,
and place me serenely
in Your presence.

 *violence*

More multiple murders.
Guns everywhere, even for children.
Resentful people turning to violence.
Comfort the families of the murdered,
I pray,
and touch the hearts of the violent.
Inspire us,
me,
to take positive strides
to halt the brutality that nourishes
our culture of death and rage.

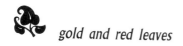 *gold and red leaves*

You must be the God of Delights,
the God of Enchantment.
When I behold gold and red leaves
fall to a pond from a blue sky,
I wonder,
"Am I not called to something
more beautiful and enthralling than this?"

my prayer

_____

_____

_____

_____

_____

_____

_____

worry

Your son counseled us
not to worry,
not to let our hearts be troubled.
When I am jobless
with a hungry family,
I'm tempted to reply,
"Easier said than done."
Infuse this timid soul
with the grace of hard trust
and blind confidence in You.

 *relaxation*

Looking out to the blue-gray horizon
on the Atlantic,
I fear I may still do everything
as if it were work—
including being away on a holiday.
Help me, I pray,
to learn to relax in spirit
and to do what should be done on vacation:
to put cares aside and open myself
to carefree moments,
all in Your sight and on Your beautiful planet.

 *suffering*

In the suffering that remains for me—
emotional, physical, psychological—
be with me.
I know You won't lead me
around the pain,
but through it.
Even so, with You at my side,
I will come through it,
even though the pain itself
is not diminished.

my prayer

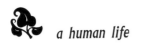 *a human life*

How old do I have to be
to learn the one thing necessary
for a good life?
It is not success, fulfillment, or even health—
and certainly not wealth,
as our culture tries to teach us it is—
but only as Jesus taught us,
the one who lived for others
and showed us what You are like
and how a human life is to be spent—
for others.

obedience

In the rush to return to basics,
to be a people of values,
inspire us, I pray, with the urgency
to be people of the Sermon on the Mount,
to let prophet Daniel Berrigan's words
seep into our souls:
"The Sermon on the Mount concerns us
here and now, or it concerns us never….
The time to obey is now."

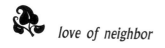 *love of neighbor*

I pray You, help me to open my heart
to true love, selfless love.
Martin Luther King
prompts me to ask myself:
Am I like the priest and Levite
on the road to Jericho
who said, "If I stop to help this man,
what will happen to me?"
Or like the Samaritan, who said,
"If I do not stop to help this man,
what will happen to him?"

my prayer

_____

_____

_____

_____

_____

_____

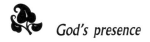 *God's presence*

As I stood by a frozen pond in the woods
as the snow fell heavily
on a windless day,
the extraordinary silence and beauty
were fertile with Your presence.
You really can turn up anywhere,
can't You?

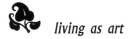 *living as art*

An artist has expressed
what may take us a lifetime to learn:
"Living is an art, not a science.
You make it up as you go along."
Step by step, we have to grope our way
in search of You,
not relying on impersonal formulas
and prescriptions,
but trusting that You,
in the peculiar circumstances of each one's life,
will lead us to You.

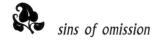 *sins of omission*

When I look back some day
in a grand review of my life,
a life abundantly blessed by You,
what will I say to You with greater urgency:
"Forgive me for all that I did wrong," or,
"Forgive me for all that I did not do:
the opportunities to love,
to make a difference"?
It's the things in life I didn't do
that I'll regret more.

my prayer

_____

_____

_____

_____

_____

_____

_____

Of Related Interest

Who We Are Is How We Pray
Matching Personality and Spirituality
Charles J. Keating

Draws on the sixteen personality types identified in the Myers-Briggs personality profile, matches each to a suitable form and style of spirituality, and shows why prayer is different for each.
321-3, 168 pp, $9.95

Everyday Epiphanies
Seeing the Sacred in Every Thing
Melannie Svoboda, SND

These 175 short reflections are divided according to the seasons of the year, and each ends with a reflection prayer. Topics range from the mundane to the unusual and unexpected and each reflection invites readers to discover God in every aspect of our lives. Scripture passages scattered throughout offer insights into the ways that Jesus used the occurrences of everyday living to reveal both God and grace
730-8, 192 pp, $9.95

Prayer-Moments for Every Day of the Year
Mary Kathleen Glavich, SND

Sr. Kathleen offers a vast collection of one-sentence prayers, organized into categories. Drawing from the Bible, the saints, and the liturgy, she assembles short prayers for every need and every expression of human emotion. Especially ideal for those who feel they don't have enough time to pray.
748-0, 80 pp, $7.95

A Prayer Primer for Catechists and Teachers
For Personal and Classroom Use
Gwen Costello

This handy little guide offers readers practical advice about ways to pray with children as well as personal guidance for their own prayer. It covers: "Your Own Prayer," "Praying with Children," "Prayer & Scripture," "Prayer & Simple Rituals," and "Year-Round Prayers for Catechists."
922-X, 64 pp, $5.95

Available at religious bookstores or from:

TWENTY-THIRD PUBLICATIONS

P.O. BOX 180 • 185 WILLOW ST. • MYSTIC, CT 06355 • 1-860-536-2611 • 1-800-321-0411 • FAX 1-800-572-0788

Call for a free catalog